Manuel de Falla

His life *&* work *with authoritative* text *and* selected music

COMPOSER PORTRAITS

WISE PUBLICATIONS

London / New York / Paris / Sydney / Copenhagen / Berlin / Madrid / Hong Kong / Tokyo

Manuel de Falla

a short biography

MANUEL de Falla is one of the greatest of all Spanish composers. He was born in 1876 in Cadiz, the seaport town at the southernmost tip of Andalucia. His formal musical education began with piano lessons, and literature was also a great passion of his early years. He established a couple of literary magazines called *El Burlón* (The Joker) and *El Cascabel* (The Rattle) in his early teens, as well as a newspaper entitled *El Més Colombino* (The Carrier Pigeon), all three publications acting as vehicles for his prodigious imagination. When de Falla was twenty his family moved to Madrid where he continued his studies with the distinguished teacher José Tragó, and composed salon pieces such as the Mazurka in C Minor and the *Serenata* (1901). He then went on to study composition with Felipe Pedrell, the teacher and scholar who had set the great revival of Spanish music in motion in the 1890s.

In 1904 de Falla won the composition competition of the Real Academia de Bellas Artes with his one-act opera *La Vida Breve* (Life is Short), and at the same time he was awarded a prestigious piano prize organised by the piano makers Ortiz y Cussó. In 1907 he fulfilled a long-held ambition by travelling to Paris; he was welcomed there by Ravel, Debussy and by Dukas, and benefitted greatly from their guidance and encouragement. De Falla's years in Paris were of enormous importance to his development — he later said that without France he could have achieved nothing. He completed several chamber works during his time there, and started work on *Noches en los Jardines de Espãna* (Nights in Gardens of Spain) before the outbreak of war in 1914 forced him to return to his native country.

His one-act *gitanería El Amor Brujo* (Love, the Magician) was a successful experiment in bridging the gap between art music and the Spanish folklore tradition. From it came the fearsome standalone 'Danza Ritual del Fuego' (Ritual Fire Dance), which inspired a further commission from the pianist Arthur Rubenstein, the *Fantasía Bætica*.

De Falla was approached by Diaghilev to write a work for the Russian Ballet and in response composed a mime-play in two tableaux, *El Corregidor y la Molinera* (The Magistrate and the Miller's Wife) which, with some subsequent revisions, became *El Sombrero de Tres Picos* (The Three-Cornered Hat), and was premièred highly successfully in London in 1919 with choreography by Massine and designs by Picasso. Meanwhile for a memorial publication in honour of Claude Debussy, who had died in 1918, de Falla contributed a *Homenaje* for solo piano. Following the deaths of his parents in 1919 he settled in Granada, where he remained until the end of the Civil War (1939), and composed several of his most important works including *El Retablo de Maese Pedro* (Master Peter's Puppet Show) based on an episode from Cervantes' *Don Quixote*, *Psyché* and his *Concerto per Clavicembalo* (Harpsichord Concerto). He then moved to Argentina and worked there until his death in 1946 just a few days before his 70th birthday, leaving the vast oratorio *Atlántida* still unfinished.

Sandy Burnett
January 2014

Published by
WISE PUBLICATIONS
14-15 Berners Street, London W1T 3LJ, UK.

Exclusive Distributors:

MUSIC SALES LIMITED
Distribution Centre, Newmarket Road,
Bury St Edmunds, Suffolk IP33 3YB, UK.

MUSIC SALES CORPORATION
180 Madison Avenue, 24th Floor,
New York NY 10016, USA.

MUSIC SALES PTY LIMITED
Units 3-4, 17 Willfox Street, Condell Park,
NSW 2200, Australia.

Order No. AM1008524
ISBN: 978-1-78305-466-4
This book © Copyright 2014 Wise Publications,
a division of Music Sales Limited.

Edited by Sam Lung.
Biography and introductory texts by Sandy Burnett.
Music engraved and processed by Elius Gravure Musicale.
Cover design by Chloe Alexander.

Printed in the EU.

El Amor Brujo

Ritual Fire Dance

I N 1914, as de Falla was busy reharmonising Spanish folk songs, he was approached by one of the country's greatest gypsy dancers, Pastora Imperio, who came from a family of distinguished flamenco artists. She asked him to write a gitanería, a one-act gypsy drama, for her, and she and her mother sang songs and told stories to him to fuel his imagination. That winter de Falla spending three months immersed in the project, holed up in a room filled with cigarette smoke and the heat of a gas fire; he'd never been happier in his life.

The great pianist Arthur Rubenstein caught one of the earliest performances of *El Amor Brujo* in Madrid in 1915; he was so struck by the Ritual Fire Dance that he took that piece into his repertoire, and it was a stunning success. Footage survives of Rubenstein playing this piece at Carnegie Hall in the 1940s. His movements are economical until he gets to the percussive passage at bar 67 when the alternating quavers begin. Rubenstein suddenly flings his left and right hands up to eye level — emulating the sparks from the gypsy's fire in a truly incendiary way.

El Amor Brujo

Ritual Fire Dance

Manuel de Falla

Allegro ma non troppo ($\quad$ = 126)

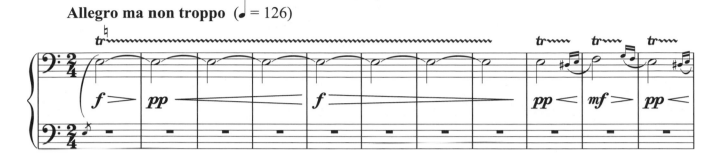

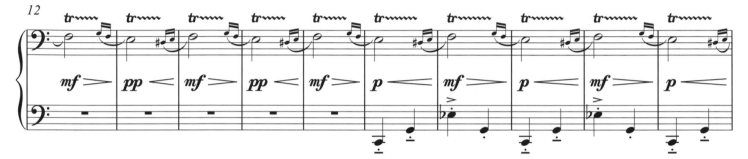

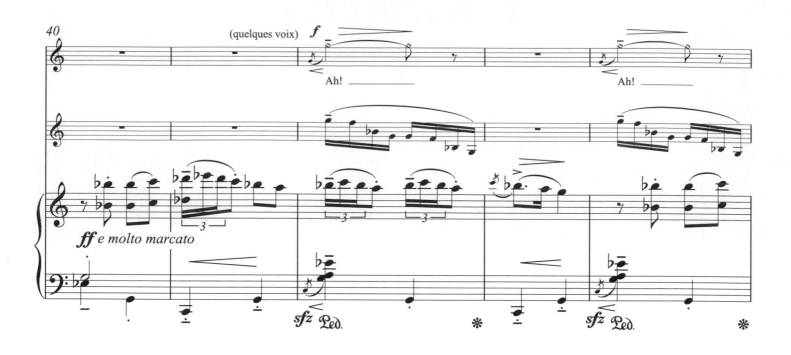

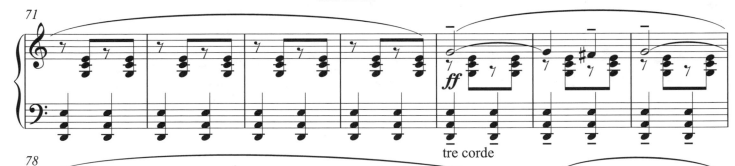

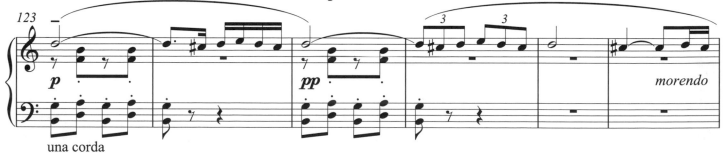

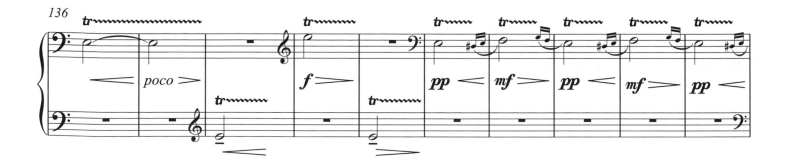

11

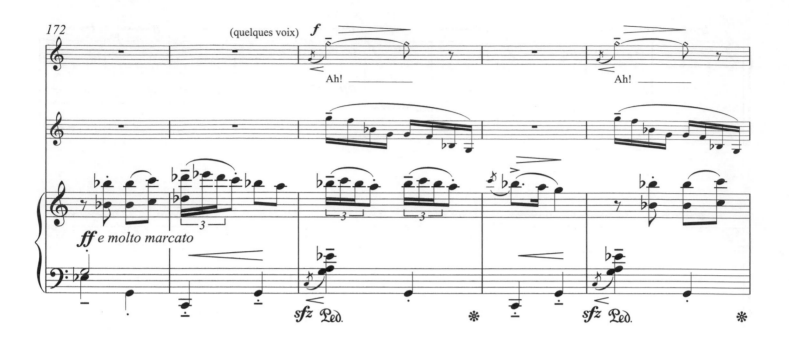

una corda

tre corde

molto dim.

una corda

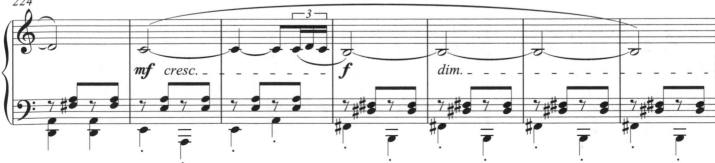

13

El Amor Brujo

The Fisherman's Story / The Magic Circle

THE first Madrid performances of *El Amor Brujo* received a mixed response from the critics, some of whom felt the music wasn't Spanish enough. But the great Pastora Imperio and the other flamenco performers really believed in the score, and felt that the music was really their own. And for de Falla, that's what really counted. Pastora Imperio must have been stunning onstage. The playwright Jacinto Benevento wrote that while watching her, 'life becomes more intense, the loves and hates of other worlds pass before our eyes, and we feel ourselves heroes, bandits, hermits, or champions, shameless bullies of the tavern…'

The plot of *El Amor Brujo* revolves around Candelas, a beautiful and passionate woman, who is trying to exorcise the soul of her dead lover so that she can move on with her (love) life. While the Ritual Fire Dance is the most spectacular moment of the score, The Fisherman's Story strikes a quite different tone. The metronome mark of crotchet equals 44 is extremely slow, its dynamic markings a picture of restraint. And once again it's worth bearing the original orchestration in mind. In the opening bars, the left hand should gently touch those staccato crotchets, while the right hand plays a simple melody in thirds that de Falla originally assigned to a pair of muted trumpets.

El Amor Brujo

The Fisherman's Story / The Magic Circle

Manuel de Falla

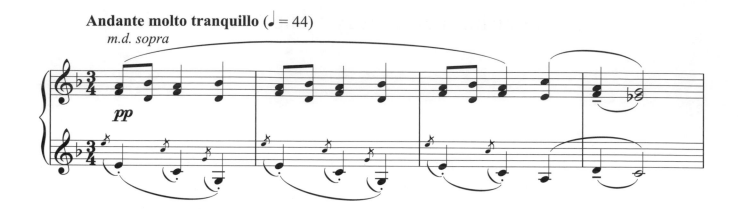

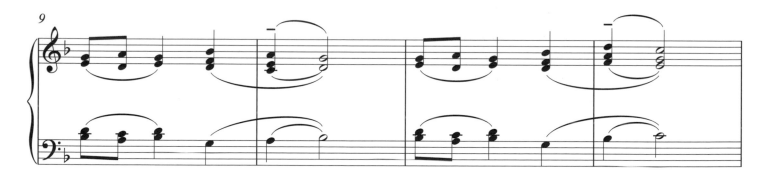

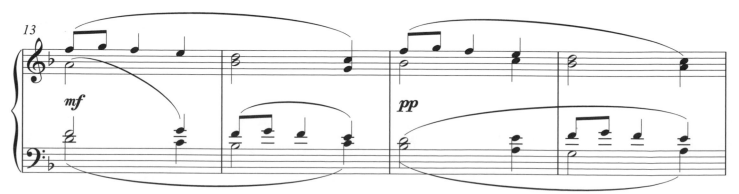

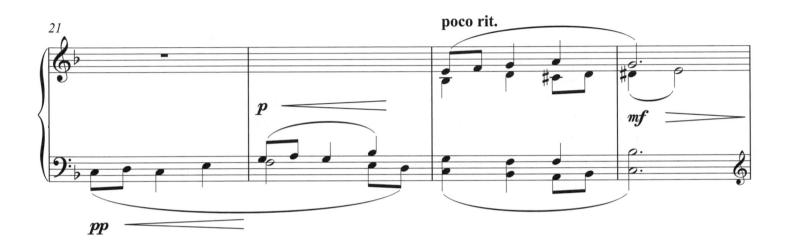

Homenaje

Le Tombeau de Claude Debussy

O F great importance to de Falla's development as a composer was the influence and encouragement of the great Claude Debussy. And after Debussy's death, de Falla was invited to express his gratitude in a quintessentially French way: by contributing to a special edition of the Parisian *Revue musicale* which took the form of a 'tombeau' for Claude Debussy. De Falla's piece took the form of a Homage — or *Homenaje* — to his French mentor. In its original form, the *Homenaje* of 1920 was the only work de Falla wrote for the guitar; he created this version for piano the same year.

Its tone is suitably sombre, with a minor key and dark sonorities. But there's also something sensuous at work too — the erotic sway of the habanera dance, which brings to mind *Carmen* without the vocals. And towards the end, de Falla places a telling quotation from Debussy himself: bars 63 to 66 quote directly from the second of the *Estampes*, 'La Soirée dans Grenade' — referencing not only Debussy's own love of Spanish music, but also the city of Granada where de Falla composed his *Homenaje*. Although de Falla didn't play the guitar, its hallmarks and techniques are all over the piece — the chord spacings, the downwards and upwards arpeggios — so in bringing it off the page, the spirit of that most Spanish of instruments should never be far away.

Homenaje

Le Tombeau de Claude Debussy

Manuel de Falla

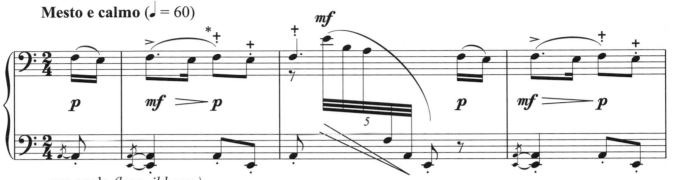

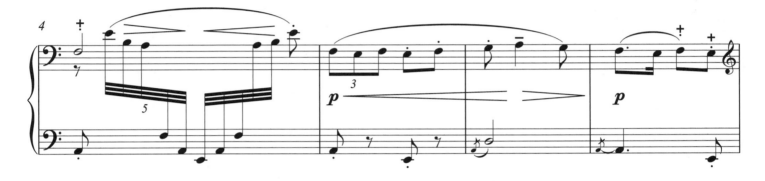

* Les sons marqués du signe + doivent être accentués, d'aprés les nuances, et très légèrement retenus.

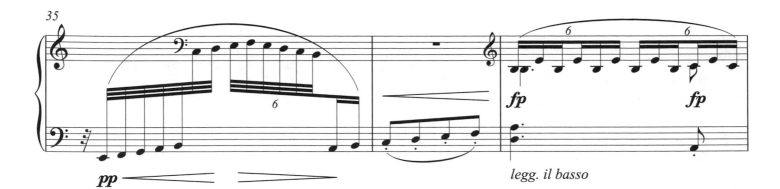

rit. poco a poco

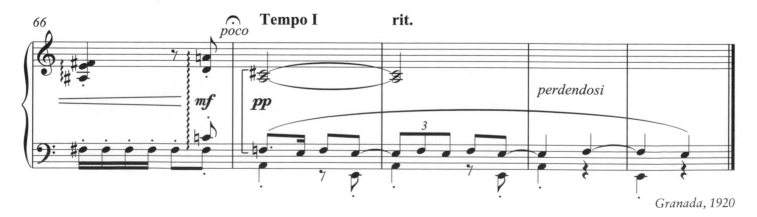

Granada, 1920

Intermezzo
from Fantasía Bætica

HAVING scored a tremendous concert-hall success with his interpretation of the Ritual Fire Dance, the Polish pianist Arthur Rubenstein approached de Falla in 1918, with a commission for a new piano showpiece with just as much impact. De Falla responded with this *Fantasía* the following year, its evocative adjective 'bætica' referring to the ancient Roman province of Iberia that covered the southernmost area of Spain and Portugal.

Rubenstein never really took to the *Fantasía Bætica*. Much of its writing is alarmingly non-pianistic, and its musical language often acerbic and challenging. Right at the heart of the *Fantasía*, though, this beautiful Intermezzo begins; its gently rolling melody is in a hauntingly Andalusian version of G sharp minor, with the flattened second of the scale making a haunting modal impact. At the opening, within the most delicate pianississimo, the main theme should be hardly disturbed by de Falla's cross-rhythms, a pulse of 3/4 gently colliding with the prevailing 3/8. The appearance of E sharps and A sharps from bar 44 raise the emotional temperature just slightly — de Falla's hairpins allows this to come through — before in the closing bars calm returns once again.

Intermezzo

from Fantasia Bætica

Manuel de Falla

Andantino (♩. = 52)   **(poco rubato)**

ppp *dolcemente marc. il canto*

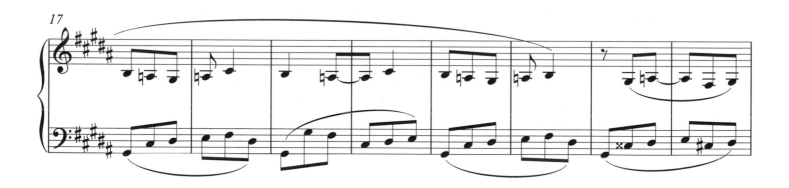

poco più sonoro

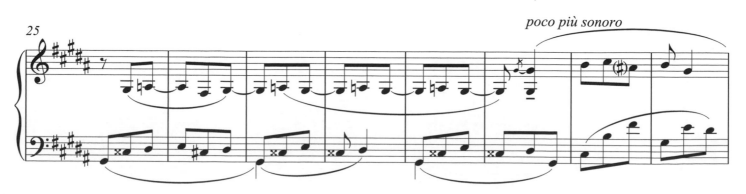

poco affr.

pp

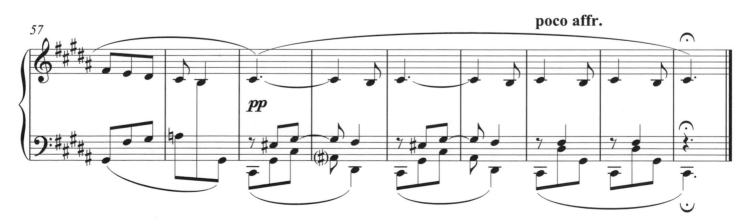

25

Mazurka in C Minor

LIKE Felix Mendelssohn, de Falla was one of those brilliant children whose creativity could have taken him in a completely different direction. He loved words, had a fertile imagination, and set up two magazines and a newspaper before his eighteenth birthday. But music had always been a passion. De Falla had made his debut on piano alongside his mother in his home town of Cadíz at the age of nine, playing a piano duet arrangement of Haydn's *Seven Last Words*. And his commitment to music strengthened and then became paramount in his late teens, when in occasional trips to Madrid he would take piano lessons with José Tragó, a highly respected pianist who had studied with a pupil of Chopin's.

The spirit of Chopin is clear in both the form and the feel of this early Mazurka in C Minor. Also at work though is the influence of Edvard Grieg. De Falla had heard a local orchestra playing Grieg's music in Cadíz, and was struck by its character and its harmony. The experience left de Falla with an 'intense desire to create one day something similar with Spanish music' — which is exactly what he went on to do.

Mazurka in C Minor

Manuel de Falla

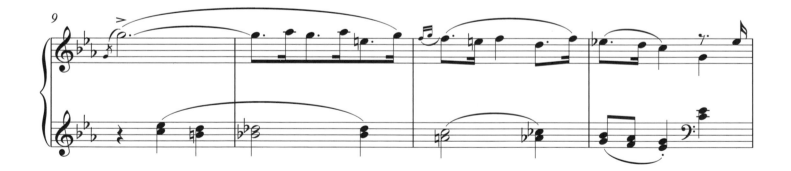

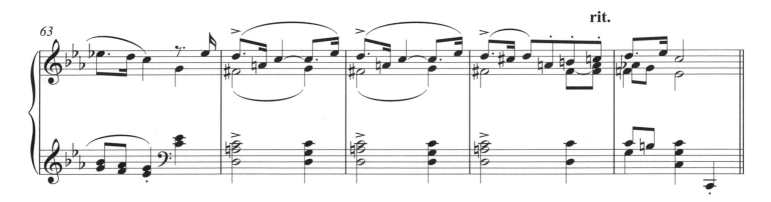

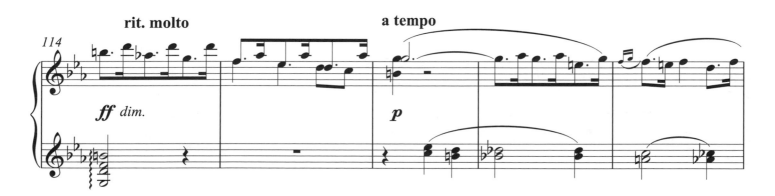

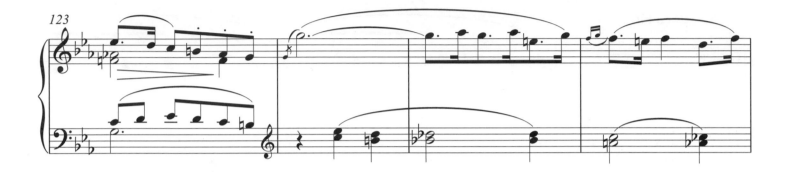

Melisandra

from Master Peter's Puppet Show

I N 1919 the Parisian patroness Winnaretta Singer gave de Falla an unusual commission — a new piece for her private puppet theatre. He responded with a puppet-opera based on the perfect passage from Cervantes's *Don Quixote*. At Master Peter's puppet show, the Don watches as the fair Melisandra is being held prisoner by King Marsilius. Never a great one at distinguishing fantasy from reality, Don Quixote leaps to her defence; he draws his sword and smashes the puppet theatre to pieces.

While much of de Falla's score is bustling with action and colour, this movement is an oasis of calm. It describes the unhappy heroine standing at her balcony and longing for freedom. While the Spanish rhythms are clear on the page, the overall effect should be linear and impressionistic. It's worth bearing in mind that in each appearance of the theme in his original version, de Falla varies the orchestration — muted trumpet (bar 1) giving way to flute (bar 5), followed by cor anglais with solo violin (bar 9) and so on. Inactivity is a virtue in this piece, so when dynamics do appear in the form of hairpins (at bar 20) the pianist should really make them count.

Melisandra

from Master Peter's Puppet Show

Manuel de Falla

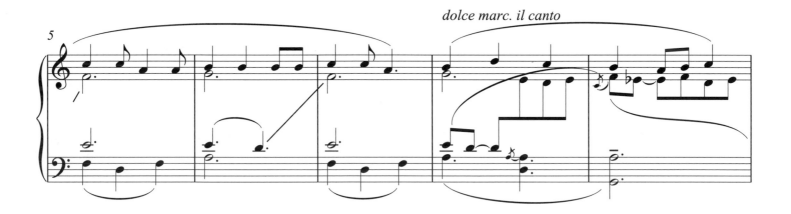

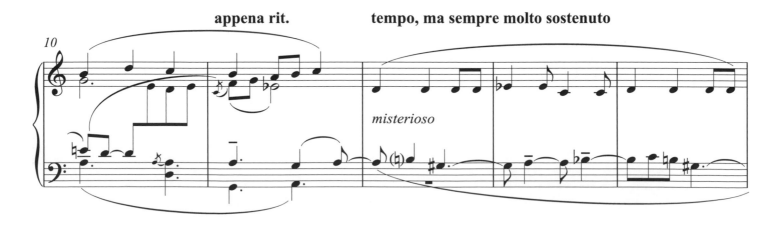

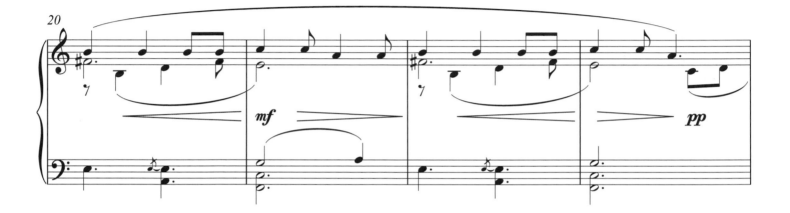

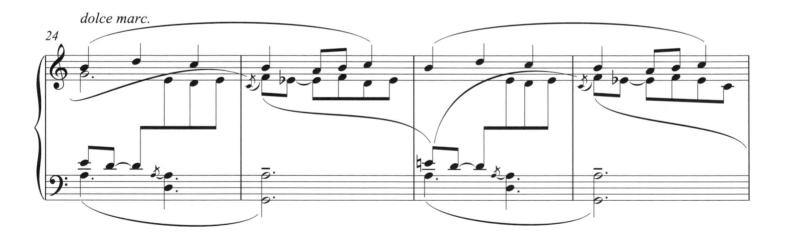

The Miller's Dance

from The Three-Cornered Hat

I T was for Serge Diaghilev's great Ballets Russes that de Falla wrote one of his most famous scores — a ballet based on the folk story *El Sombrero de Tres Picos*. Collaborating on the London première in 1919 was a real dream team: Ansermet conducted and Massine choreographed, with Picasso designing the scenery and costumes. The title describes both the three-cornered hat worn by the village governor, and a three-way amorous intrigue. The governor wants to have his wicked way with the Miller's wife, but he's frustrated in his ambition — which is partly to do with the manliness of the miller himself.

The opening bars are all about the thrumming guitars which accompany *The Miller's Dance*, which bristles with machismo, the rhythm of the fandango, and general Hispanic energy. It's important to bring out all of the dynamic variations, from the *fortissimo pesante* opening giving way to diminuendos, then the dramatic pianissimo crescendo up to a pesante statement with three fortes. No room for politeness here! The entry of the A minor theme towards the end of bar 10 needs a complete change of colour. And the accelerando towards the end should unveil itself slowly, leaving plenty of room for a scamper to the finish.

The Miller's Dance

from The Three-Cornered Hat

Manuel de Falla

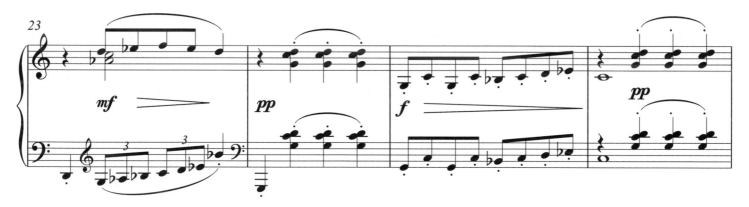

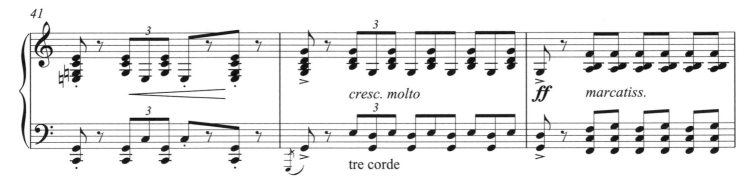

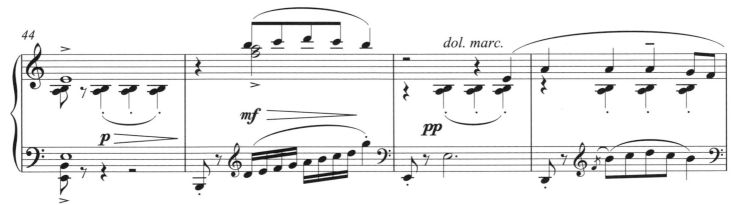

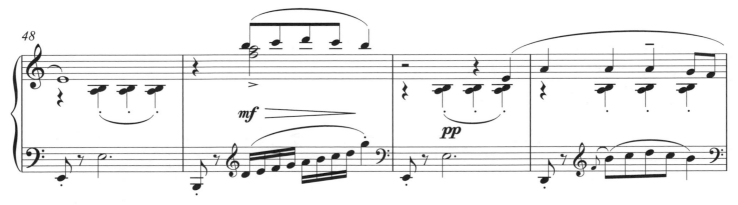

Pochissimo più mosso, ma ritmico

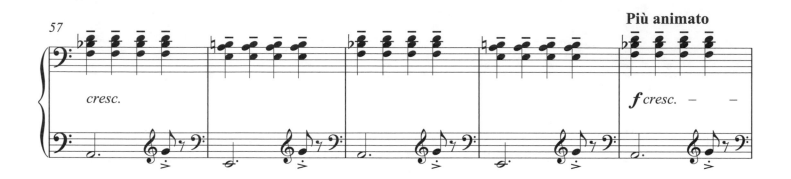

Più animato

animando ancora sino il fine

Serenata

1901

IN 1896 de Falla moved to Madrid to pursue his studies full-time at the Escuela Nacional de Música y Declamación. Things there could not have gone better for him; in 1898 and 1899 he scored top marks in all of his courses, and won every available prize. Meanwhile de Falla dipped his toe into writing *zarzuelas* — Spanish operettas — on the side as a way of making money, and began to explore his country's folk music in earnest: the folk songs of Andalusia, and the *cante jondo* of the flamenco tradition — the 'deep song' of the Spanish gypsy population.

There's still something of the salon about the *Serenata* de Falla composed in 1901 — its opening bars have a delicate interplay between E minor and G major which once again brings Chopin to mind — but the Spanish influence is perceptibly growing. De Falla makes greater use of the Spanish language in his performing indications — writing *sentido*, or 'with feeling', as the central section begins at bar 51. Gently arpeggiated octaves from bar 156 bring the guitar to mind, while de Falla brings his serenata to an end with a flamenco flourish; two staccato crotchets, to be played firmly, within a pianissimo dynamic.

Serenata

1901

Manuel de Falla

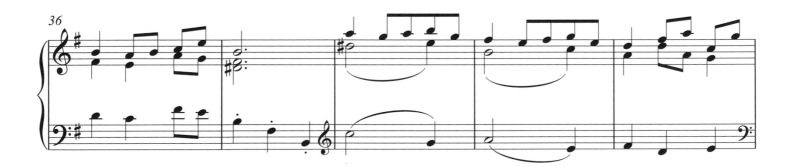

poco rit.　　　　A tempo, sentido

Como al principio [Tempo I]

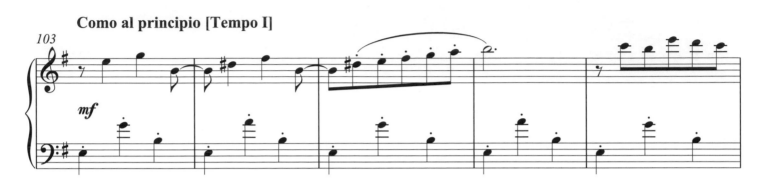

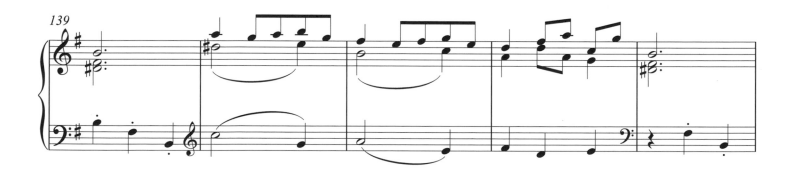

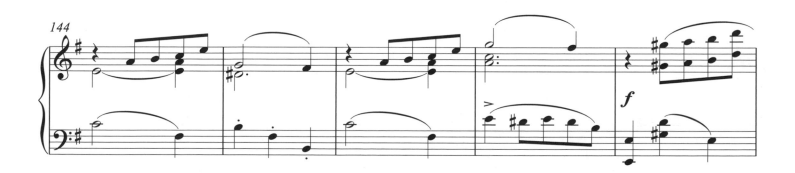

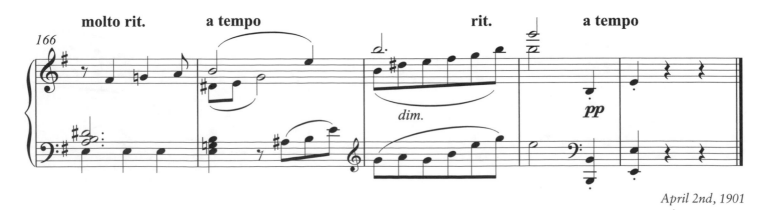

April 2nd, 1901

123456789